COLORING BOOK
and REFLECTIONS for
SOCIAL EMOTIONAL
LEARNING

James Butler, M.Ed.

ILLUSTRATED BY
Becca Borrelli

free spirit
PUBLISHING®

ISBN: 978-1-63198-533-1

Free Spirit Publishing does not have control over or assume responsibility for author or third-party websites and their content.

Cover and interior design by Shannon Pourciau
Edited by Cassandra Labriola-Sitzman

Printed in the United States of America

Free Spirit Publishing
An imprint of Teacher Created Materials
6325 Sandburg Road, Suite 100
Minneapolis, MN 55427-3674
(612) 338-2068
help4kids@freespirit.com
freespirit.com

FSC
www.fsc.org
MIX
Paper from
responsible sources
FSC® C005010

Free Spirit offers competitive pricing.
Contact edsales@freespirit.com for pricing information on multiple quantity purchases.

ACKNOWLEDGMENTS

I would like to thank the following people for their support, wisdom, and guidance: Lindsey (best partner ever) and Theo (best dog ever); my former students from Winn Elementary, Barbara Jordan Elementary, T. A. Brown Elementary, and Gullett Elementary in Austin, Texas, and from Mangetti Combined School in Mangetti, Namibia; Becca Borrelli, the amazing illustrator of this book; Austin ISD (AISD) superintendent Dr. Paul Cruz; AISD director of race and equity Angela Ward; AISD director of SEL Pete Price and AISD assistant director of SEL Caroline Chase; my awesome AISD SEL teammates; Laurie Grossman; Donald Altman; Manchester University; Alyssa and Judd Absher; and my family (especially Grandma and Grandpa Butler).

—J.B.

I would like to thank, first and foremost, my family: Jason, Layla, and Rose. I would also like to thank art teacher extraordinaire and forever mentor Andrea Schepis; my former students from Woodland Elementary and Highland Elementary in Stow, Ohio; Meagan Whiteley for buying me my first adult coloring book; Tara, Ryan, Elliott, and Hannah Clifford; Emma Borrelli; and my parents, Wayne and Margaret Borrelli.

—B.B.

This book belongs to _____ .

Use positive self-talk while drawing pictures of yourself in the frames. For example, breathe in deeply and think "I am." Breathe out and think "kind." Continue this breathing while you draw.

I AM KIND

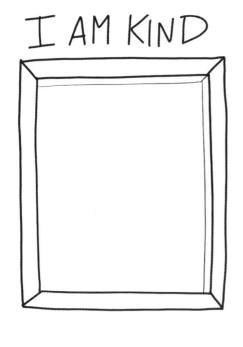

I AM STRONG

I AM SMART

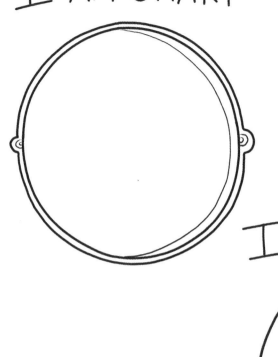

I ♡ MYSELF

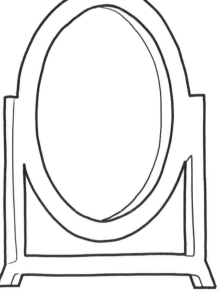

NAME YOUR FEELINGS

It's important to name your feelings to help
yourself and others understand how you are doing.
What feelings do you remember having yesterday?
What feelings do you have right now?

What feelings do you notice in this illustration?

MUTUAL RESPECT

Mutual respect means treating other people how you would like to be treated. Why do you think mutual respect is important? When can you show mutual respect?

How is mutual respect represented in this illustration?

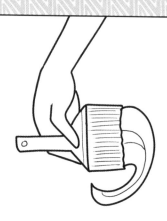

INCLUDING OTHERS
Including others is a form of showing compassion.
Have you ever felt left out? How did that feel?
What can you do next time you see someone being excluded?

How do you think the character with long hair feels about being included? How do you think the character with the glasses feels about including others?

ACTIVE LISTENING

Active listening is listening with your ears, eyes, mouth, heart, and whole body. What does it mean to listen with your eyes, and so on? When can you actively listen?

How is active listening affecting the characters in this illustration?

WAYS TO PLAY FAIR
Three ways to play fair are play together, trade, and take turns.
Can you think of any other ways to play fair?
What is a situation that would require playing fair?

What examples of fair play do you see in the illustration?

COMPASSION
Compassion is kindness, caring, and willingness to help others.
When have you felt compassion?
What is a situation where you could show compassion?

How are the characters showing compassion?

COURAGE

Courage is the strength and ability to do something that frightens you. When have you felt courageous? What is a situation in which you could show courage?

How is the fish showing courage?

SELF-TALK
Self-talk is positively talking to yourself about your choices or how you see yourself. Examples: "I am strong." "I am smart." "Should I do this?" When could you use self-talk?

What self-talk do you notice the character using in this illustration?

SPEAK UP

It's important to speak up when you or someone else is being treated unfairly. Have you ever spoken up for yourself or someone else? When could you speak up?

What do you think the character with the megaphone
is saying to speak up for the character in the hat?

HONESTY

Honesty is being truthful no matter what. Honest people gain the trust of those around them. What is a situation where you've had to be honest? How can you be honest?

How does this illustration represent honesty?

BEING A GOOD FRIEND

Having good friends is a key part of life that requires acting with mutual respect. What makes your friends good friends? How can you be a good friend?

How is the giraffe being a good friend?
How do you think each of the friends feels?

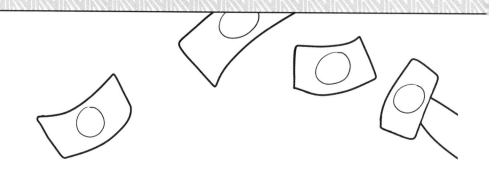

INTEGRITY

Integrity is making good choices even when no one is watching.
When have you shown integrity?
How can you act with integrity?

How is the dog acting with integrity?

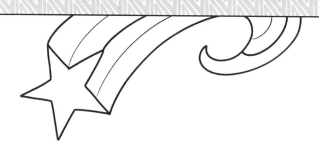

BELIEVING IN YOURSELF

It's incredibly important to believe in yourself to achieve
your goals. When have you believed in yourself?
What is a situation where you need to believe in yourself?

How does the unicorn see itself in the mirror?

LEARNING FROM MISTAKES

Mistakes happen. They provide opportunities for growth if you learn from them. When have you learned from a mistake? How can you learn from mistakes?

How does the illustration show what the character learned?

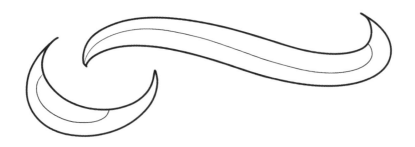

GRATITUDE

Gratitude is being thankful and returning kindness given to you.
What or who are you thankful for?
How can you show gratitude for what you're thankful for?

Why are the flowers grateful?

GENEROSITY

Generosity is showing kindness to others through actions, service, or gifts. When have you felt generosity? How can you act with generosity?

How is the squirrel with the acorns being generous?
How is generosity affecting the squirrels?

SELF-COMPASSION

Self-compassion is loving yourself and giving yourself kindness.
Why do you think self-compassion is important?
How can you be self-compassionate?

How is self-compassion represented in this illustration?

POSITIVITY

Positivity is focusing on goodness and happiness in your world.
Why do you think it's important to be positive?
What positive things or people do you have in your life?

How are the characters showing positivity?

SEEKING HELP

It's okay to seek help to solve a problem (after trying to resolve it on your own or in an emergency). When have you sought help? When is a good time to seek help?

How are the characters helping each other?

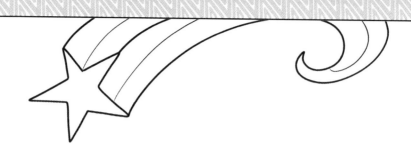

PERSEVERANCE

Perseverance is continued effort to do something even when it is hard or takes a long time. When have you persevered? How can you show perseverance?

Why will the character need perseverance?

ADAPTING TO CHANGE

It's important to learn how to adjust to new life/routine
conditions. When have you had to adapt to change?
What could you do if conditions changed today?

How did the butterfly adapt to change?

EMPATHY

Empathy is understanding and sharing someone else's feelings.
When have you felt empathy?
How could you show empathy for someone today?

How is empathy represented in this illustration?

SAYING PROBLEMS WITHOUT BLAME

Saying a problem without blaming someone else is
a problem-solving skill. For example, avoid saying
"You always . . ." and instead say
"It makes me feel _____ when _____."
How could you say a problem without blame today?

How does this illustration represent
saying a problem without blame?

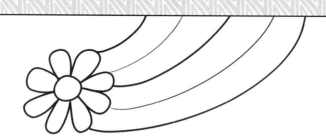

STRONG FEELINGS

It's okay to have strong feelings. It's important to manage them appropriately. When have you felt strong feelings? How can you calm down when strong feelings arise?

What is the character doing to manage strong feelings?

COURTESY
Courtesy is being polite to others and showing good manners such as saying "please" and "thank you." When have you been courteous? How can you show courtesy today?

How is courtesy affecting each of the characters?
How do you think they feel?

PATIENCE

Patience is remaining calm during difficult situations.
When is a time you have had to show patience?
What can you do if you're in a situation that requires patience?

How is patience represented in this illustration?

FORGIVING OTHERS

Forgiveness is when you let go of negative emotions about something that happened. When have you forgiven someone? What is a situation where you can show forgiveness?

How has forgiveness affected the character with the heart?
How do you think forgiveness could help the other characters?

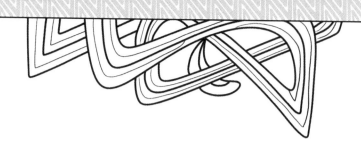

ANXIETY/WORRY

Anxiety is feeling worried about something.
When have you felt worried about something?
How did you deal with it?
What can you do to calm down if you feel anxious?

How is the character managing anxious feelings?

RESPECTING DIFFERENCES

Being different from others is beautiful. Our differences
make us unique and special. What about you is unique?
What can you do to respect people's differences?

How are the characters different?
How are they respecting each other?

CARING FOR THE EARTH

We only have one Earth and it's ours to share with plants,
animals, and other people. How have you taken care of Earth?
What can you do to care for Earth today?

Why are Earth and the other characters smiling?

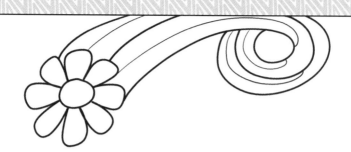

TAKING RESPONSIBILITY

It's important to take responsibility for our actions and not blame others for our decisions. When have you taken responsibility? How can you take responsibility today?

How is the elephant taking responsibility
for its actions by helping the flower?

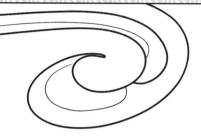

BEING A TEAM PLAYER

Teams aren't just for sports. You can think of TEAM as
an acronym for Together Everyone Achieves More.
When have you been a team player?
How can you be a team player today?

What are the benefits of the crayons
working together as a team?

PUT-DOWNS

Use your words to stand up for yourself and others when
put-downs happen. When have you dealt with a put-down?
How can you handle put-downs in a peaceful manner?

What do you think the mouse is saying to the cat?

TRYING YOUR BEST

Always try your best. No matter what. Nothing is possible
if you don't try. When have you tried your best?
What is a situation where you can try your best?

How is the sun trying its best?

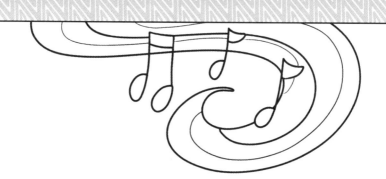

HAVING FUN

Have fun. Smile. Enjoy yourself. Life is way more enjoyable
when you're having fun. What is a time when you had fun?
How can you have fun today?

How are the characters having fun?
How do you think they feel?

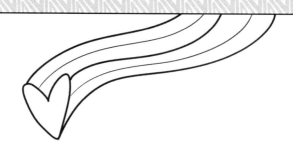

TAKING IT HOME

We learn a lot about social and emotional learning and mindfulness in school, at home, and out in the world. You can use SEL and mindfulness in all these places. What lessons have you used with classmates? With friends? With your family?

What is the importance of using social and emotional learning?

SUGGESTIONS FOR USING THIS BOOK WITH CHILDREN

Coloring Book and Reflections for Social Emotional Learning was written based on my fourteen years of experience as a classroom teacher and two years of experience as the Austin ISD SEL mindfulness specialist. The social and emotional learning (SEL) topics and reflection questions were taken from my book, *Mindful Classrooms™: Daily 5-Minute Practices to Support Social-Emotional Learning (PreK to Grade 5)*. You are welcome to use this coloring book in conjunction with the educator guide or by itself. It can be used in the classroom or at home. However you choose to use the coloring book, I suggest that you engage with children about the coloring and reflection questions.

The thirty-six SEL topics in this book represent the thirty-six weeks in a school year, if you would like to space them out like that. You can use them in the order presented, or hop around as topics naturally arise. Each topic has two pages. The left page is for reflecting through writing or drawing; the right page features an illustration for coloring. This was done intentionally to represent the more logical left side of the brain and the more creative right side of the brain. On the next page are five suggested activities for each SEL topic. I recommend spending at least a few minutes on each activity.

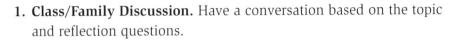

1. **Class/Family Discussion.** Have a conversation based on the topic and reflection questions.

2. **Reflecting on the Art.** Each piece of art has a question connecting the art and the SEL topic. Guide children to reflect on the art by thinking about the question. Discuss their answers together.

3. **Mindful Coloring.** Take some time to color. Guide children to bring their attention to the coloring. If they have thoughts arise, they can gently acknowledge the thought, allow it to pass like a cloud floating by, take a deep breath, and return to coloring.

4. **Journaling.** Have children write or draw responses to any or all of the questions on the reflection (left-hand) page.

5. **Reflecting on the SEL Topic.** Ask children to quietly reflect or lead them in a class/family discussion about the work you've done surrounding the SEL topic.

For more information on my mindfulness resources, including the educator guide *Mindful Classrooms*, visit freespirit.com or email help4kids@freespirit.com.

ABOUT THE AUTHOR AND ILLUSTRATOR

James Butler, M.Ed., is an author and the SEL mindfulness specialist for the Austin Independent School District (AISD). During the 2016–2017 school year, he helped implement a mindfulness curriculum in all 130 AISD campuses. He is the founder and owner of Mindful Classrooms™. James lives in Austin, Texas. Visit his website at mindfulclassrooms.com.

Becca Borrelli received an M.A. in Art Education from the University of Texas and currently works as an art teacher at The Contemporary Art School in Austin, Texas. Visit her website at beccajborrelli.com.

◆ ◆ ◆ ◆ ◆ ◆ ◆ ◆ ◆ ◆ ◆ ◆ ◆ ◆ ◆ ◆ ◆

Other Mindfulness Resources from Free Spirit

Interested in purchasing multiple quantities and receiving volume discounts?
Contact edsales@freespirit.com or call 1.800.735.7323 and ask for Education Sales.

Many Free Spirit authors are available for speaking engagements, workshops, and keynotes. Contact speakers@freespirit.com or call 1.800.735.7323.

For pricing information, to place an order, or to request a free catalog, contact:

**Free Spirit Publishing • 6325 Sandburg Road, Suite 100 • Minneapolis, MN 55427-3674
toll-free 800.735.7323 • local 612.338.2068 • fax 612.337.5050
help4kids@freespirit.com • freespirit.com**